WS' all t's

harry k stammer

Sandy Press

walls't's, by harry k stammerr

Cover design, cover preparation,
& interior layout
by harry k stammer

ISBN: 978-1-7368160-1-1

Printed in U.S.A.

Sandy Press
Queensland, Australia
&
California, USA

https://www.sandy-press.com/
sandypress@gmail.com

A

pants short

ripped knee
stained "I picked the
shit off"
(taped hair) roll'd
directions there
fold "onto my shoes" drip to drip't sensing't
ambush ambush am bush bush bush bush
dare'd dare'd dare'd
playing
"uh, one more" tender (forget) time a

soft (er) tune
sung
"haul away.."
ambushed'd mention
the dare

groups

"the ending is dense"
invisible (me)
line(s) foggy
smooth'd sur (face) 'nt't
"there in back
pattern one'd little one
(hold can't) mountain top
sense (s) anger
'itter 'oilet "joke" (ing)

this glass
inside climbing hand up
(touch) paint
"are out,
now" hole tiny like't
middle fore finger
pad (rub)'t over
"do you need an outlet?"
inside "i don't know"
little't hole rubbing
over't skip

the target

blacks (up) to "are you?"
false
front (s)
"no, what?"
white run up
(says) down (to) slipping (road) icy
"Tom?" do
you "is he..."
us both side'd
(time'esqu) thirty degrees
yours "that cast call"
peppers nose's

check'd rubb't
theirs (oranges apples tissues)
"best of them"
till tongues hang
(lime tree)'t
press one eye
behind
"the screaming"
thought't
2 five and 7 five ten

busy (sun)

up (fog) 'gy
"look, mom!" there
wall brick steps
(since) titillating "you know?"
plays cost
"shall"
found drip'ing set
"love to
leave" bacon "a friend"
loving swear flat wall against (me)
move 'ring 'ead
'old 'nemy (a)
context or people some (real)
"really, real!" attribute or
'ribute
"mercy!"
shake't (it) speaking it "no, no"
farther (to) fish "dang it!"
(farther) section off now

sparkle "ere?"

photos (tongue like)
hanging up "again,
I don't's know 'ere?"
spinning (lower throat)
drip expect'd in April
"ere?"
sticks snowing't at
"his pen, he really doesn't use it much"
ready yeah

dumb
"a little painting"
you've unknown fight'd gun
boom boom boom - paste (t)
less lit
(gray'd) eye piece
'here lying set (per) punding
flooding (a) tale setting (sun is) saying
"bath, baby, oh"

do this "to a country"

smell't (uh'm) check
"say, four weeks"
spray it (oh)
buckerooo's
bread (flour paste)
this (done or done)
table
two pipes
"attached by screws sets's"
one place to another
functional (real) less (ly)
hand table strap (ed)
triggers's 'orgot ('ndisipline)
"thank you"

alarm ringing
out (the town)
step'd glass
"piece (ing) it
back"
realistically knife top
(wooden) tipping boat (s)

another puncture wound

(three inches)
severing two tendons
vessels drain'd
"against more bricks" waiting into
'ergence re-make
lack'd directly's
"don't poke it"
too
much (spent) it
"don't poke it"
again 'ailed massacre't since

"we just walked in"

fun fun lotta (go)
"of course"
'ignal (to) sound'd
throat center
back rubb'd (scratched)
'eaching placement
"check the table"
chair back (see)

the fun fun lotta (go)
depressed in the lining
page to page
(pictures's) arm
here leg there
"jump up there" strings (ing)
spot ceiling
wax'd under tire
'ravel (go) 'densation
"coming back
down"
smaller hole drilled
to 1/8th inch 'in liner

front grill

two books
"a spring in hell's"
but don't but
(elbow to elbow) crawl
sweaty and sweating
through linked (fences)
two fingers
pulling second (metal) 'alad passing
"hope I'm not a"
monkey (men) mention'
one to four
drum't (people)
die't 'vryday evening
"mostly, I didn't hear"
your (exposure'd) connection
"let us know why..." forth
so spoiled and
"a medium size carrot, please"
remaining

"turn it into"

skip (ing) fun (did) you
breaking as pole
"let's break"
older doubt
less
"searching for the shore"
(best) water lines
dangerous (door)
hard (oak) knob
turned'd in bump (ed)

"you don't slide"
finger'd (he)
said I (said'd)
check (it) "you buy it't"
3 six
nine (spine) "look, David!"
chiseled't round (d) back
walking I stepped
into the field
knees wet's
er

connection buried

(sunscreen'd)

"blathers now, sickness"

people to

pairs two sections

lean (ing)'d

"that bumpy stucco

scratched's"

push up off the

sidewalk (waking) tire water

"ssshhhhhh"

over pulled finger

'cross paper crackle't

stepping back

the ruler cross'd

"where's the room?"

(my) arches

dragging a'sock stuck

"where's the room?"

tents (grounded) shutter

open "do you see it?" case first

first (mention) single

finger prints cycling

"where's the room?"

"you don't drop"

shortage's (s)
"just (the) because
you didn't" asleep?
(on bottom) submit rapid
(ly)'s "it's socialism and
they're trying to scare
you" parked next curb

ants climbing over't one leg
48% working
here set set'd
olives dropping sets
step two feet
"bet it's only one"
do scaffolding baked'd lymph
(node) liquid's eaten on
ripped "look!"
hair hair hair
circumference ant line moving't

"don't drop it?"

just tell her (!) toes
lines 'onfirmed "cause..."
if you do thank
(me) Tuesday p/u another
down spout spider pulling
bloddy fingers's
between's (as)
razor edge 'orn 'mer 'ock
broke the
window (hand)
knuckles "that pair of
doves lives"
making do hit (me)
"it's
their, men"
soon (er) gone space
thumb fore
(finger)
"don't kiss him, anyway"
honey oh (oh) slice't

clicking (clickiting)

‖ : call : ‖
pair off "now!" up
sun trees's
"make some eggs"
seen surgery
a'role (mountains)
"so strong it'll kill'ya"
high (baby)
rip it open - two bags (filters off)
Doritos's 'licking more
(a) riot thrown
cabbage
"who throws it?"
shape't
now (now) "you can sing it."
machine't
flake (off't) resting
"hang it" on'a
'exval (since)
sense (reveal't)
"in a tree" it works

strickin'

"don't steal" life (real)
positive x-y "you
over there, hey asshole!"
little nap (asleep)
in a bag (for) 'a moment
"it's over
here"

chocolate cake (;)
see'ss revolving "not a put..."
"there's a back way in"
stones (up against)'t
'play "to it."
real (life) it alive
(it's) "back way" 'ward bathroom
drowned another disso'
piling (on)
two by three
"I'm on five, Frank!"

deals "sit down"

again (here) wonder(s)
belt'd safe
(ly) "I don't know?"
printed'd weak probably
sake (a) hash't
choked "do you?" dead't into
arranged soon
1 x 3 (tiny)
rocks larger sooner't
"you got black glasses"
caring (caring) grab "on
your forehead"
one leg stuck (sticking)
"howdie, partner'd"
crying (a couple)
alone't singing barely
zero reset (mama)'s
paying tonight (isn't) free town

legless "you said it"

once grounds (drained) floor
wall (spider)
"not what you though"
bending
one (out) of "ways"
model had "boys, less"
show under
"one speck" (ing)
company deform (ity)

haven't
sunshine (temper) "ear mark't it"
one nose bent
inner (voice'd) test'd
"mama kissed it" debate'd
sunshining (not relent)
ing not
"daddy rubbed it"
dragging a bag (rocks)
'nitial to fore (private) door

doorway 'solved

"tracking two now" touch knob
cold (fig.) 12 less a (1/4 inch)
an inch this
'way two lines away from
crack ninety degree move
(lining) growth't
cold copper less
"you can't portray it"
like wall (face) 'ed back
back steps

(smashed eye) anchor "like that"
like't 'entury cart'd away
"anymore" a slap and'a
face "ok?" trio (split'd)
 lit'd "yes, three is the number."

four 'seminal its

(a) make considered 'tional in
non 'tary flesh
melts hot iron
masque "sizzzzzzzzz..."
small amounts and
'fusion
each little (bug) round four 'minal
(no one) as zipped
numerous thick's
rounded "just pour it"
swarmed'd
scant 'ful "any how"
'rity "my finger
aches"
(just) forgot "drink?"
words advil another
'ping "hello?"
moment (I wish)
grounds moved low (er)

clearly focused

"into a few days"
everyday that
baby forward out
element "by the areas"
seconds "ill take two"

cause your brow (right)
one (looks) a day or
a few ahead less bits of steel
epi' centr'd
"he isn't ill"
seriously (remote) ramp
ramp ramp gap'd
"now" no time the
course'd
"step over it" get good
"never!" count down (t)'s
'enter'd's "and"
middle positiveness 'n'sure

absolute pictured

face scratched'd

fence sooner blessed (ed)

certain'd "you know, clear..."

feet/foot dark (ness)

"smells that foggy" edge

wise over five thousand

examples

resolution source

"drag them over here"

clear 'ing

"you can always drop theme off"

over there

limbo take't (to)'esque

linked "into the

slot" sanctuary (les) 2 more

"drop them" on

the floor 'over't backed

into "again" 'gainst

and again (you)

agreed coughing

"took the train" looking
'ternally "can
it" more scratch (ing)
head rocking between
shoulder roll't (regular)
combing hair "sip it" out
seizing't around (and)
"through a straw" clump'd
back 'n forth
tight shrunk showing't

along with "how to tie
that" showing "a parade"
have (ing) talk
stuck'r stopped at (self)
"don't forget to set't"
wipe't contact "and lift"
to do belt'd in pull

"needy bastard!"

destitute (humble) man then 'poverished left
"low class, asshole!" tumble'd down the hill
sweater pant a belt "what did it mean?"
sleep sleep bend tooth picks (front) "that his teeth (is)"
"take a trip" point'd trouble get out of

town (out) of't to town (while) express'd

blue't yet "I'll get my hair done" in
where (in) "Tulsa?" two rooms one bath take one

"you learn your nouns"

learn (ing) verbs
attempt'd
background the
pine needles the tiny leaf
debris "since it's"
two 14 plus (babies') "when
a crack"
place it "appears again"
twelve 'n four
[Jack] plays't along
"glistening blind your" [Jack]

playing sun (less)
foot inner 'leeded brass
hat'd thigh "and blind (ly)"
awareness (choices) yet
"focused in't" bare forehead
(into) rub rub't
memory more

headaches (four)

explosion "spikes of light" drum (ing)

"as if a" thought(s)

interest'd less

"bomb

went off'a"

set the table forms left knives

right'on and glasses (flown) street

(ing)'t fly

over scarce

sound numbers negative

"you said it was red"

honest (gained)

seen (it)'t prepare-it talking

"segue, there"

no talking here-it's agreed

"when you

back out"

light no

nodding there it

was "back there"

my only friends

"pack it up, the car" speak
a towel
a brush
a cigarette a
bench't driving 1 A.M.
(Mojave) melting 1 dry
"do we (really)
know you?"
rip rip rip
"tug" July 1st beef (on)
pizza ground by
the dozen (pants) and peck
peck peck
"drop" singing "it"
droop leg over
over over fall't (ing)
as "open eyes" think (?) wink

B

bore (dom)'t

"break't am" pissing wall stripe'd for

"on hours, see"

tunneling (ing) 'ing slot

(ed't) freedom's clouds (a) and'a

someone "who knows"

vision (ion)

specific (pain it)'t

look

"it's twitch'ing" ever object

pee'd on wall

long red stripes (a) a

finger scratching

"I love you" napkin back

(that) wallet's picture(s)'s

placed "let go of what?"

that brick someone's slab't

drool(ed)

mask of (slender) legs

induce infuse

(d) "a lot about"

dead line

(s) there attract'd (d) back smaller than

"you" you

(tamp it)

less (when)
"feel the change" rattling
pocket (s) "it's a bisquit"
a tower't
(of't) piece't it
plays "come on" flex't
solid (hand)
to and two digit
knuckle (place) nail
charging
into this door
"put it" key clank't
knobs "no suction" bugs
on the floor
you (that) squeak as squeak
opening slowly (lack)
"that you" took (bait) plus metal
clip "could see"

"could not"

little bombs
(fusing)'t burn't eye cornea
(oust)'y tongue lick
(to the wall) L.A.
smell (83)'s nosey
(ah'up) "ten cent coffee?"
it
a

the as is (toes)
"always, honey oh" twelve
signatures's better
feet slide't dragg'd ankle back
heels
click (clack) hard
wood(s) "pale skin" [gray]
confuse'd and depending
hesitate blank out "afraid
of a repeat" a sea (s) rolling
puzzle's of your
(in vulgum)

plug hot (=)

penis' (some)
one "ten minutes"
weave based door "differ,
 you're forgetting" left
just fix't (drift) bent down
eyes down down
sets "drifting in an ocean" lean
over matter (s)
target paper trace (up)'t
"damn nose hair" and
the cat (where't) window open
"yeah, yeah,"
the bird bath 'race
planted point and sharp
manu (-facture) of't memory
(s) lift up
the brick

he looked

(pale) or ticking
since noon us
taken orally (oral)
support mouth roof razor
(less) a (a) -a grope (grope) "hey is
your name...?"
'parently center white line that shadow isn't
brink dragging
"in from the snow" them living
(in) room(s) apart "and, hey?"

going
where "came back" hands (out) file (ing)

step the paring
one potato (grunt)
less just over the

"could not" back inside

"though, bet?"
poolside pre- (salad) sets
up't will (shoot) pack't two socks a
shoe "a little pebble" move
screen'd over asphalt rock

"that corner" light

blink (across) one body left
leg (in) now
"do the same" part
(it in) middle lapping "come over here"
incubate tongue (s) lick (ing) eggs
are not here
flea (s) (and a)
hornet "that added &
as" frogs (leaving)
four holes (tiny)
"burrowed
line" half (too) train'd
training on going light
(d) 'rop 'tense "don't pretend"
wiping off counter lips

pressed

forward (think) dripping
(ing)'t deal't at one
(tales) feel (away) "still, I think it's
up" prick (a) little one -back (select) "you
were the one, babe" lips (stick't) out'of less (s)
pink
shrouds wave
(y) member (milieu?)
nail pull
't back "if you look at it"
claiming
clanging 1 or 2, 3 (4)
through the

shoe stepping (of)
"not of the" the'the same'same it

"i thought it was over"

plant your ass
(down) here
"isn't a piece of shit"
bunch up (rope)
'less shouldn't "you ok?" when
bunch up (sheet) 't more
"take it" the (you)
that disability
(that song)
sing (ing) motorcycle
ghe'ee'ee pull back the chairs
(and) skip (a tune)
screaming't wheelspin'
"grab the beer, ok?"
don't (t) ok alone (me) works

pack the bags

take a shit eat some
toast
"broke my nose last night"
my
nose (set stone) curb
red "the less" water
flail (ing)'t down face'd
thresh swamp smell (er) back
fog mist brown
slug (g'd) pit
"in the" sun
light (famous) fire
"where the smoke" going
(ing)'t
finger tip trace't (the)
gravel line
begin
(s) and't (an) ash (es)
twirling in't (dis) charge

dipping 'round "take a right, here"

got had
to (soaking)
"we're going east" under the
problems
"the other one"
sentence (less) er (a)
tend (tender) "help!"
tending't sell it (!)
sell sell
hug (a) mail (man)
"you can sentence him"
sandals
dirty choices
"little'drible"(er)
curb
big wheel measured
miles (in't) out silvery
ribbon
box sent wrap (up
"you see that water?
now't

breakfast "right?" try

(yes) it's
drone un
d'drone't gone
(outer)
"left, no leave"
talk protect blank't
two eggs' pancakes
bacon -coffee potato (s)
(s)
bell pepper red sauce
"leave left, no"
say (ing)

alone (back lean'd)

doorway left "enter right" donut
wrapp'r (that diabetes) "next to sugar" particle
"there's a"
planter't
weedy elbow 'less ex-
old (pebble'n)
trench'd san (y)
'le 'le 'le 'le
birds barks

"those mockingbirds, fuck!"
any where walk
(ing) about'a about "course't"
fit much at
singles
"not 'tth" blame (is)
blue "eyes on
my baby"
bark't want'd where't 'lipping
track'd across

afraid 'p 'p 'p

"see me?" - -
- (lit) ('it't)
'lace push "the gravel
is hard"
'ward lack'd pair'ing
one want'ing wish
ing't "jump on the boat"
'asking'ing' two
fingers up
"windy night, huh?"
bait the (fish) bunny
backed
forward wheelbarrows stuff't
a place a place
terry cloth (many) question
'ex 'the'd lax "oh,
yes, very windy"
backing (ing)'t eyes
(steal't) punctures

C

room not open wooden

dowl stuck (under) "what
is the matter?" Rosalind looks (like) "those
are cabbages
by the road" on the field (....) marked
(....) marked

square door (wide)'r open 'siveness
outdoor (fears)'t 67 (degree)'s
shoe hole wet as
water "walking through't" there
rock a'buried'd sparrow
(set)'n wake'd robin "a fog" hard forget (d)
one over hang (left)
wing less "a rain" (s)

drop the book

(finger't)
say's affect "let's walk
outside"
toe step
glass
clk clk nose
in the
carpet
"can you see the tree?"
blade'd (pairs)'n "no, not a thing..." pegs (a bunch)

tried

"fifty years old"
to phone (blue'ish) set
"say chrome"
walk (ing)
suck't't 't 't
"n' mean?" go lets (episode)
bright 't and
(a) forget sand shoe
(trend) going
through little finger
protect buckets
(protection)
"in the details"
musty taken
oak table (shatter(ed))
"paragraph 12"
pages glass
pieces oak floor (etch'd)
nail red (ish) (no
please)
'ense's splinter'r 'el 'on'ray
"details, like" it

"you just jumped"

planter dirt mouth't (past tensed)
it (buta-buta) mixed
"look"
two triangle 'played
sugar
"lips, wait for me"
just drop it't
-pair 'igure'less "like a boat mooring" twelve (saintly)
drugged

treble horn straight

(section) step to step'up 't

clang (iron) fractions"this is on isn't"

failed will (will)

"whether playing"

brick brick brick

though another (bricks)

focus'd "or not" trouble with not

chains

link a fence (dawn)

track track (say)

it's cracks (concrete(ed))

"you and Joe!"

take (this) tap toe's knocking

(a) door survive (al)

"do not know" upset (one)

balling bouncing

least bounce

question one

coali-tion 2nd Ave.
"you've got 6th"
around the pole
(sign)
[the birds nestle
in for the night]
"now 7th" turn't
asking
for someone
shoulder's 'ension
talc powder (grant'd)

distrust (irony)

"forget the play on words"
watch
(background) the hat
(fixed)'t us morning
rows bottles "words"
crazy (clean) 'rule
that (high)
wall back to (alley)
"words" hush'd low
long brick

sad
(objective) "in the immediate area"
left leg
a stump reflect "a hub cap" nothing
"for at" seventy year (so)
"you get' movie that feeling it" 's
(soap) wash wash 'et
while here

dropped in (two stones)

"where've you been?"
something
clicked (a beetle)
an insect (pair) it
(up) the middle (4 stones)
second tick 'a 'a 'a
"are you ok?"
step toes first
(river/stream) rocks

pipe "yeah"

red flag (baby) sprouting "a red

flag"

twist't cement 'ncircled't

(drop) by

two

poles red flag (baby)

sprinkling't whether broken knuckles

"yeah, it's"

big book (s) red flag (t) 'ain on us

"want to"

products six rubber-ize't

(smiling) "go out!"

lips to (service) mud (mud)

"now it's

time!"

audio (problem)

product(s) silk (fiber)

"time

to!" backed rubber

(yellow)'d take (a)

shit'd on the

ticks one clock two

"turning 40's"

groups wallet

(s) "buy some new teeth"

motion "murder

your mother!

burst pipe

(except)

"that broken heart"

thrown stomach up

(another) tick (an) 'piece

"take brillo pad to your shins!"

singing
make me stop't
a 'ground a notch street
"buzz words, sit"
frankly (1) equal x^2 stairs
leading up "my
bags don't fit"
sorry it's squeez'y
bought three more
"taste it..." forget
'xlan floor 12
more "light lime..."
check't silver pipe'd (ceil)
ing (more) "salty pears"
pant spotted miss (ed)
"place the gun on the ground"
heard both meant't

treble't

 again two ants
(walking) shortn't was
problem'a clear (er)
treble'd print card (I'm)
"get a job, asshole!"
corner screeching bunny dead
(treble't) squared times
four feet "don't slip on the blood"
exhaust "grab that"
aperçu fades buried (never) push
"it's two blocks down"
'recho (now) soap

bar
"wax it down"
trade a bottle (during
milking) later (the)
frost lawn stick (greeks')
don't point

decline (raising) 'd

knee leg [as] "the drapes
are blue"
'stinct wall [was] "like
a certain hue"
several (mistakes)
[were] soft a
'ield(ing)

"you'll see't"
elbow [at] "on the floor"
pumps (up) basic
"you put it" [like] a
pumps work
"over the fence"
a selection
(n) a
"dump it'a" [so] was
"flimsy, etc."
pump't rk'
row (man) row
"so, so, so" so

pure

"don't mix it"

radio [lick] sounding't

quiet

tires rain

and (few) lights

"stay with

me"

purer (as)

licks muddy brick

(engine's) beat

reflection'd water

"hear that violin?"

up [ink]'t flat

sparkly

cross't and stupefied head

(slung) down [was]'t low
fingers tapping tap,tap, tap't, ta singing
"don't drown me" table tap, tap't "out, now"
honeys home (a) when't you look'ta sing "baby" less
everyone (says)'s moments "sentences are longer" 'cupation and

switch
the hinge (er)
say(s) "moments in
here"
combined'd 'matic'd back (for)
"tiny pebbles"
'band'd
[door] (sighs) finger
(door) [sighs's] a (and'a)
says everyone

"nuts are candy"

blight like (very)'s range
"yet not" one more room (bed) it's
floor where (dresser) "so turn" suffering crab

cake like "I'm your inmate" (s) tender pales here

rheumy sadness (eyes)

mother "wait in"
run (the)
forget (get)'d
"just a bet" two water
out's flow't
"that will be"
two 'percolate sand
(s) drill'd turn'd
"scorn me if you"
must't
putt't
the hall long door
way "sense it..."
easy wanted "no...!"
scene trial'd
"no potential,
no" knee
to knee hand to hand (le)
an opening (der)'t
whether course
vary (s) "yes"

spread'em "fine"

selection't shuffle (ing)
"the ring doesn't
seem to fit"
construct'd
(pale) moons played
47 degrees/s
"can you pick another one?" punch
down (o)
"the other lamp"
please more seen tell

another angle plug't

china and (see?)
been't not
store'd (but)
"you gotta beer?" no
side
still generous "in India?"
(of the) last
week drawing in [Thailand]
and (not)
"do you hear that?"
bark bark bark
minutes (too many)
another word
barkbark
"an elevation that takes into
account"
window (and)

tomorrow'd divide't immersed
saying "yes"
slip shoe (backwards)
"maybe right"
shave't pare them again

"the politics here"

no reason's's graying
at "are
you stinky"
shining within (being)
"and blus't'ry"
sun spokes (water)
knees facing winds
"page eight"
peeing in the ocean
(over) reflection and windows open

"charge it"

present where corner sidewalk wall meet
"don't get all..." past (against) nothing (in
the) shadows's twisting 'round "worked up" click click
click walking "and get out of the way" mockingbird chimney
burned

two arms (bandage)
"you this ooze?"
lock'em <exit>
"it's the government" paired 'ith
'ere section
'nal sofa (s)
"no, I don't!'
plow't under (rows)
each one tagg'd "issues, you" then

[cane thuds]

skid't "brush the plants"
dust'em corner
window (corner right up)
tremble (tremble't) shiver
shivering't staircase red lines
(step up) [scoffs] "the
coming after creates a load of leaves"

skip down

harry k stammer lives and works in Santa Barbara, California.

Other works by harry k stammer

tents - Otoliths (Lulu)

grounds - Otoliths (Lulu)

tocsin - Otoliths (Lulu)

sidewalkss - Concrete Mist Press (Amazon)

tocsin poems #1 and #2 - https://harrykstammer1.bandcamp.com/

ah